Best Wishes for

Mary Anne Denhoon

Aladin Seminars
4408 Roland Ave.
Baltimore, MD 21210

AS YOU WISH

Carol Gates &
Tina Shearon

Published by LifeSuccess Productions Inc.

Published by LifeSuccess Productions
P.O. Box 54291, Phoenix, Arizona 85078
800.871.9715   800.317.9679 (fax)
www.bobproctor.com

Cover Design: Britt Asbury
Inside Design: Patti Knoles

Printed and bound in the United States of America

ISBN 0-9658133-1-2

ACKNOWLEDGEMENTS

There are so many we would like to thank who have provided incredible leadership/ mentorship in the area of conscious, positive living; however, the list would be too long. Specifically, we both want to thank Bob Proctor for his invaluable and incisive teachings on the power of the subconscious mind.

We also wish to acknowledge some truly wonderful women who have provided unconditional friendship and encouragement: Kristin Roehmer, Elyn Nicholson and Renee Cermak.

To our husbands, Mark and Dan, we thank you with all our hearts for your adoring love, unwavering support, and room to grow. You are amazing men.

Love and Light,
Tina and Carol

DAY ONE

For eight years, Hannah's daily morning routine included a stop for coffee on the way to the office. It was just one of the many unconscious activities which occurred in the course of her day. In fact, her entire life was lived on auto-pilot.

Divorce papers changed all that nearly two years ago. Suddenly, nothing about her life was either predictable or safe. Despite the heavy turbulence, Hannah kept her shaky plane in the air, hoping to rise to the higher altitude of a better life for herself and, most of all, for her son and daughter. Then, just a few weeks ago, she uncharacteristically accepted an offer to transfer within her company and moved more than a thousand miles due west with her twins and all their earthly possessions.

And so it was that on this first day of her new life, she ventured into Storytime Café, the morning gathering place of choice among the El Deseo locals.

Friendly faces turned toward her as she entered. She was greeted by the owner of the café, an energetic young woman named Aimee, no more than twenty-one or twenty-two years old with blonde hair and pretty blue eyes that sparkled - even from a distance. Hannah had a passing thought that someone, perhaps Aimee's father, must have set her up. How else could a woman so young own a thriving business like this? And with Aimee's looks, Hannah speculated, it was no wonder the place was so busy. She mentally drew a conclusion, "Some people are born on Easy Street. I was born to struggle on my own!" ⌐ "As You Wish!"

Just inside the door to the left was an old-fashioned service counter with barstool seating. All the way to the right at the other end of the shop was a simple raised platform, a stage of sorts, with nothing on it except an old upholstered bar stool and a microphone on a small table next to it. The rest of the room was a collection of twenty or more small round wooden tables with two or three chairs at each. Only a couple of tables were empty. Hannah chose one near the window on her right.

At precisely seven o'clock, Hannah learned the reason for the name of the café as an attractive, vivacious woman in her early fifties entered and walked directly up to the platform, seating herself gracefully upon the barstool. The chattering voices grew quiet as she held the microphone to her mouth and began telling a story without an introduction.

Once upon a time in a place far, far away a quiet gem named Aggie lived in a cave high up on a mountain. She loved her cave life very much. It was safe to live up so high, though it was often lonely. Other gems also lived in the caves up on the mountain, but they kept to themselves. One day a stranger came. She said her name was Pearl. The local gems were stunned by her luminous lustre, so they welcomed her at first. Then Pearl told them about a big water down below. She said it was bigger than the mountain. Aggie couldn't believe her ears. "Water? That big?" she scoffed. "No way!" How could that possibly be? The other mountain gems laughed at the stranger's nonsense and returned to their caves. However, Aggie courageously stayed and listened. The stranger said, "You must come see it for yourself. I'll take you there today."

So, off they went. Aggie was more excited than she had ever been before, and she was also quite afraid. Soon she saw the vast water. Boats of all shapes and sizes stretched as far as she could see. Some had sails, some had motors, and others only oars. Then Pearl told Aggie that she owned her own boat and sailed it far and often.

"Oh, I'd also like a boat all my own," Aggie gushed, "to take out on the waters." And so they went down to the dock and inquired about the price of boats.

Hearing the prices, Aggie was afraid, "Oh, dear, I've never spent that much before. I'm not sure I should." Then the boatman told her that she could choose from three different kinds, which he would gladly show her.

The first boat was small and empty except for a comfortable-looking seat in the middle. He explained, "This boat is remote-controlled. You get in and someone on the shore moves it for you. Aggie's eyes grew wide and she shook her head. "No, I don't want a boat someone else controls. That will never do," she said.

The second boat also had a comfortable chair, which was placed in front of a computer screen. The boatman explained that this boat had pre-set programs which would take you to a certain point and bring you back to where you started. Again, Aggie shook her head and said, "Oh no, I don't want to be stuck on the same track doing the same programs over and over. That will never do."

The third boat was filled with gear – ropes and oars and sails. It even had a motor. The boatman beamed and said, "This is the best boat of all. It goes wherever you want, as fast as you want, and in any kind of water. You only have to know what you want, and it will make it so." And then he warned her, "This boat costs much more money."

Aggie's heart raced. She'd never thought about spending so much money, and she had never come so far from her cave. She was more excited than she had ever been before, but she was also quite afraid. She searched in her pocket and counted the money she had saved for years. She had just enough. "Yes, I want this boat," she said. "I'll take it right away!"

And so Aggie got into her new boat. Her first command was, "Up sails!" and up they went. Then she said, "Sail fast!" and fast they went. She said, "Anchor here. I want to swim." The anchor dropped overboard, and into the water she went. Then a gem she had not seen before swam over from a different boat, and they played together. They swam around Aggie's boat making circles in the water. They dove deep and swam back up, happily gasping for air. They laughed and danced in the water. Then her new friend swam back to her own boat and they both waved and sailed away. Aggie said, "Go *home," and the boat returned her safely to the harbor.*

Aggie was elated about her experience and returned to the mountain to tell her friends about the wonderful boat she now owned. She told them that she had named it As You Wish and that she had sailed it far out on the great water, which was called the Sea of Emotions. Her friends were afraid and turned away from her, which made Aggie very sad. She did not remain on the mountain very long. Yearning to explore more, she sold her cave. She returned to her boat, which became her new home. And, adventuring far out upon the waters, she lived happily ever after.

The storyteller, Genevieve, stood and bowed as she placed the mike down on the table. There was a polite round of applause. Then the café crowd casually resumed their conversations. Hannah was quite touched by the story and the poetic telling of it.

As Genevieve walked past her table,

Hannah said, "Thank you. That was lovely." Genevieve smiled warmly, "You're welcome. I'll see you again soon, I'm sure." Hannah nodded, hoping that she would indeed see her soon.

Hannah arrived at her new office prepared for a day of continuous interviews in the quest for employees who would staff the new eldercare facility that was under construction in the valley. Her responsibility for the next sixty days was to recommend the hiring of health care professionals, housekeepers, a recreation center director, a restaurant manager, and many other auxiliary staff workers.

Hiring and managing personnel was an ability that came easily to her. Although she was often told she should start her own business, she was much too afraid she'd fail, thinking, "I'm not smart enough to run my own business! I don't have the time or resources! It would be a total disaster! I could never do that!" "As You Wish!'

At noon she took a break and lunched alone in her office. Her thoughts wandered back to just a few short weeks ago before the move to El Deseo. She had felt miserable and stuck in her life. One day as she sat in her old office staring out the window, she declared, "I am ready for a change!" *"As You Wish!"*

A week later change came. Hannah was offered the opportunity to transfer, all expenses paid. Although it seemed a huge move, she told herself, "I wanted change, and here it is. I can handle it." *"As You Wish!"*

So it was that the power of a sustaining thought born of a deep desire gave her the courage she needed to move her family across country. It was the first brave thing she had done in over two years – in truth, in all her thirty-three years of life.

Hannah was grateful that her twins were enjoying their adventure. That morning they had climbed on an ancient

yellow school bus at the end of the street
for their first day of school. She admired
their tenacious spirits, thinking to herself,
"New beginnings are easier for them than
they are for me." ⌞ "As You Wish!"

She finished her lunch and prepared
herself for a full afternoon of interviews.
At three o'clock Hannah discovered that her
next appointment was actually with the
storyteller from the café that morning.

"Hello, Genevieve. I'm Hannah, please
have a seat." She motioned toward a chair at
the round table in the middle of the room.
Hannah was immediately awestruck by the
expensive pendant Genevieve was wearing at
the base of her neck – a dazzling diamond
encircled with precious gemstones. She wore
matching earrings and a fabulous diamond
on her right hand. Hannah found herself
thinking that this woman hardly seemed to
need a job!

Genevieve broke into Hannah's
musings, "I'm pleased to meet you, Hannah.

I recognize you from the café this morning."

"Oh, thank you. I'm sorry that I was staring. Your necklace and earrings caught my attention. They're absolutely beautiful. Someone must love you a lot to give you such exotic gifts!"

Genevieve chuckled and replied, "Actually, I enjoy the pleasure of buying what I want simply because I know I deserve it. These were, in fact, a present to myself which I purchased in Italy on a spontaneous little spring adventure with friends."

Feeling a little embarrassed, Hannah quickly turned the conversation back to the interview. "Oh! Well, they are stunning! Let's see. It says on your application that you're interested in creating a part-time position as a Storyteller at the eldercare center." She looked down at the form, not sure what to make of this odd offer from such an independent woman.

Genevieve's voice was warm and

friendly as she explained, "I love to tell stories - real stories and make-believe ones. Storytelling is a disappearing art form, a hobby I find soulful and fulfilling. It can also be quite entertaining."

Hannah was intrigued by Genevieve. "I'll see what I can do." she said, "and let you know." With a handshake and a friendly smile, Genevieve got up and left.

Hannah returned to her office and looked out the window just in time to see Genevieve driving out of the parking lot in a sporty blue convertible. Hannah marveled at this woman's style and flair, thinking, "What a lucky lady! I wonder if she's married or divorced, or if she was widowed young? Well, girls like me have to work hard to earn a living." "As You Wish!'

That evening after work, as she pulled into the parking stall of her modest two-bedroom apartment, she braced herself for the demands of her pre-teens, Aaron and Andra. She knew they would be wound up and excited about their new school, new friends, and new life. Exhaling a long, deep sigh, she proclaimed to herself, as she usually did at the end of the day, "I am so exhausted and overwhelmed."  "As You Wish!"

Before opening the car door she whispered aloud into the ethers, "I could really use a little help here."

In that very same instant, just a few deep breaths up the mountain, a dazzling flash of light burst from the center of the scenic meadow at High Ground. Pulsing and prancing with grace and delight, Genie promptly replied, "Ahh, Hannah! Your thoughts are my commands - you choose your every gift. I never call it good or bad, it's always As You Wish."

In a whirling, swirling dance of lights, she whisked off into the Valley.

DAY TWO

The next morning the twins and Hannah were running late and bumping into one another in their little apartment as they prepared for their day. She glanced at her checkbook balance in frustration before tossing it into her purse, thinking, "This is all the spending money I have left until payday." *"As You Wish!'*

As Hannah was walking out the door, Aaron rushed in to say, "Wait, Mom, we have to turn in our field trip money today!" Hannah dug into her purse and looked dismally at her cash on hand. "How much is it?"

"We have to turn in ten dollars each."

"Well, I only have twelve in cash. I'll write a check."

Andra came in just then. "NO, Mom! We're supposed to bring money! We'll look stupid if we bring a check! How can you not have twenty dollars?"

"I never carry much cash on me, that's all."

"Why?" Andra demanded. "Why don't you ever have money in your purse when we need it?"

Hannah grew impatient. "There isn't an endless supply, you know. Money is hard to come by." *As You Wish!'*

Aaron added with a smirk. "Not for Daddy. He always has money in his pocket whenever we need it."

Hannah was angered by the comparison and snapped at Aaron, "That's enough!" Then, in a softer tone, she offered, "I'll stop at an ATM and drop the cash off in an envelope at the front desk with the school secretary by lunch time."

The twins flew out the door in a huff as they saw the bus pulling up at the end of the road. Hannah sat in her kitchen awhile, quiet and deep in thought. As irate as she felt at their outburst, something in their words rang true.

It was too late to stop at the café, so she settled for coffee in the office that morning.   Between interviews and meetings, she found her mind wandering back to the conversation with Aaron and Andra. She was edgy and agitated all day.

That evening, after the children were both sound asleep, Hannah's thoughts returned to Genevieve's story of 'Aggie and the Boats.' So much about it made her think. And remember. The story tugged upon her mind and heart with a strong sense of familiarity.

Suddenly she raced over to the drawer where she kept her dream journal. Flipping frantically through the pages, she found what she was looking for. Dated almost two years earlier, she had recorded this dream:

Several families are on a small lake boating, swimming, and playing. I'm alone in a little boat without oars or motor. Someone is causing it to dash rapidly from one end of the lake to the other. This makes me nervous. I look over at the shore and see the outline of a figure who is using a remote device to maneuver my boat. I call out in distress, expressing concern that people might get hurt. The figure ignores me. I feel helpless. I want to row my own boat.

Hannah was mesmerized as she connected the dots linking that dream and Genevieve's story. What a disturbing coincidence. "What's going on here?" she whispered. "I'm so confused." She went to bed that night in an introspective mood.

In that very same instant, just a few deep breaths up the mountain at High Ground, Genie sighed into the meadow, "Ahh, Hannah, Listen! Hear your thoughts, hear what you say. It's always As You Wish."

And her whirling, swirling dance of lights whisked off into the Valley.

DAY THREE

Hannah awakened late following a fretful, restless night. Andra and Aaron were up and ready to go as she wandered into their tiny kitchen.

Before leaving, Andra hurriedly reminded Hannah, "Don't forget that Aaron and I are both sleeping over at Brad and Natalie's house tonight, so we're going home with them from school which is SO perfect 'cause Natalie's really neat, and her mom, Margaret – her good friends call her Maggie – is really cool and Brad and Natalie have three other little sisters and remember there's no school tomorrow because of a teacher's meeting, and so we can work on our class project 'cause Natalie has her very own video camera, and they live in a perfect house with a gigantic yard, so don't forget to drop off our stuff at their house on your way to work, and ... "

Hannah teasingly cupped her hand over

Andra's mouth in the middle of her run-on sentence. "OK, OK, OK. I got it. I'll do it. Just make sure you call me tonight."

Watching her children run excitedly down the road to catch the bus, Hannah murmured to herself, "If I had married Mr. Right, then I would have a perfect life like Margaret. Some women have all the luck. Not me." *"As You Wish!"*

She felt the walls of the apartment closing in around her as she finished getting ready for work. She knew that she had set aside enough savings to purchase a home in which they could be much more comfortable as a family. Briefly, she considered the possibility and then shuddered at the idea of such a giant financial commitment. With a wry smile she said aloud, "That's certainly not a risk I'm ready to take!" *"As You Wish!"*

As soon as she had the car loaded with Aaron and Andra's gear, she headed to Margaret's house, which was in an exclusive gated community just outside of town. Hannah parked in the circular driveway and was about to ring the doorbell when a bright, smiling woman dressed in workout clothes opened the front door, "Hi! You must be Hannah! I'm Maggie! Come in if you have a minute. I just finished with my trainer and was about to have coffee."

Hannah was amazed at how fit and trim Maggie looked despite having five children. "Actually, I have to get to the office," she said.

"Well, they can wait a few minutes so we can visit, don't you think?" Maggie insisted.

"You don't work, so you probably don't understand," Hannah replied. "I really have to be there on time for my boss."

Maggie was kind with her reply, yet straight to the point, "I work more than you might think."

"Oh, I'm sorry about how that sounded. That's not what I meant." Hannah rushed to explain. "I'm sure you have a lot to do, I just mean that you are fortunate enough to have a husband who works so you don't have to. I mean, have a job, that is." Hannah was only making matters worse with every comment.

"That's OK, I know what you meant. Maybe you'll have more time to stay when you come back to pick up the kids." Looking at Hannah with a penetrating gaze, Maggie went on to explain, "I would love to tell you all about my business. My office is here in my home. It's become a family project, as a matter of fact. My husband handles all the accounting and enjoys working from home, as well."

Feeling a little embarrassed, Hannah's response was awkward, yet sincere. "I'll look forward to that. Maggie smiled and waved her hand as Hannah made a quick and speedy exit.

At the office, around ten that morning, the receptionist buzzed Hannah to say, "Genevieve is here to see you." Startled,

Hannah quickly said to send her in.

"I wasn't expecting you today."

"I was in the area and decided to drop in. Do you have any news in response to my offer?"

"Why, yes, the staff loves the idea. In fact, I'll put you together with the new director next week." Hannah was tempted to tell Genevieve about her boat dream. "I really enjoyed your boat story. It reminded me of ... well, of some memories of my own." She was hesitant, though, and too shy to continue, so she deliberately changed the subject and asked. "Do you anticipate any conflicts with your schedule at Storytime Café?"

Genevieve assured her, "Oh no, there are no conflicts at all. I offer my talents freely to Aimee. It has always been a service rendered strictly out of friendship to help grow her new business. In fact, Aimee's older sister, Maggie, is one of my best friends and a business partner in

several other ventures. I'll be going now.
I look forward to hearing from you soon."

After Genevieve left, Hannah sat back
in her chair with a puzzled expression on
her face. She could not picture such a mis-
matched friendship. She would never have
guessed that Genevieve, the spiritually-
grounded Storyteller, would be close friends
with the entrepreneurial socialite, Maggie!
And more odd, who would have imagined that
Maggie and Aimee, the young coffee shop
owner, were sisters? Nothing seemed to fit!
Hannah allowed herself to be caught up in
her thoughts about these uncommon women.

For a fleeting moment, Hannah put
aside her judgments and acknowledged her
longing for friends like these. She looked
at the papers piled on her desk, however,
and reminded herself, "I have to work and
raise my children. I don't have time for
friends!" "As You Wish!"

That evening the apartment was
unbearably quiet. Hannah realized, tossing a

frozen dinner into the microwave, that she had become a loner with few outside interests. The twins had been her refuge from the world. And now they were growing independent.

Feeling bored and lonely, she remembered something she had seen on a TV talk show. She picked up a pen and blank page of paper and said to herself, "I'll see if I can think of ten things I'm grateful for ... well maybe just five!" She began to write, and the list grew. Two hours and one hundred-two treasured items later, Hannah drifted off to sleep.

In that very instant, just a few deep breaths up the mountain at High Ground, Genie blew a goodnight kiss into the air saying, "Ahh ha, Sweet Hannah. As you wish! I'll see you in your dreams!"

And her whirling, swirling dance of lights whisked off into the Valley.

DAY FOUR

Hannah awoke with a start at four forty-four in the morning. She switched on the light, took out her journal, and in a hasty scrawl wrote out a strangely exciting dream:

I see a beautiful, large, round drum. It is the only image in my dream, and it's set against a black screen. It is golden brown and has an ornate wooden drumstick lying next to it with a strong triple-braided cord attached. I want desperately to strike the drum, yet it remains just beyond my reach. I continue to stretch and strain and eventually grasp the cord, pulling the drumstick to me. I strike the drum with one powerful stroke. The sound is amazing, deep, and melodious. I am exhilarated and thrilled by its vibration, knowing that I am capable and abundant beyond my wildest dreams!

Hannah struggled to grasp the meaning of her dream. She sensed that her dream was something terribly important, not to be taken lightly.

Staring at a blank page in her journal, she suddenly saw her entire life played out like a motion picture on fast forward. Now and then it stopped in a freeze frame, and she would stare at a mental photograph in time. Then she'd go spinning forward once again, reeling from the awareness of missed opportunities. Her mind flashed from one scene to another, playing out the series of photographs that made up her life so far. She was tired of being alone.

Hannah showered and dressed quickly, racing to get into her car and be out among the living. Looking at her watch, she saw that it was only six o'clock. Hannah decided to go to the Storytime Café and pull herself together.

She ordered a double espresso mocha at the service counter before taking a seat at the little table by the window once again. Hannah was visibly distracted, almost angry. Aimee, who was sharing a table with Genevieve, went over to deliver Hannah's order.

Genevieve had been observing Hannah closely from the moment she entered the room. She saw the confusion and distress playing out in Hannah's eyes and was intuitively moved to reach out and be a friend. She walked across the room and asked, "Hannah, do you want to talk?"

Hannah gratefully did just that. She told Genevieve all the details of the last few years, her fears, her divorce, her disappointments, her anger and her blame. She was drowning in resentment, and it felt good to vent.

Genevieve listened patiently until Hannah paused to rest, then she asked, "Hannah, what do you want?"

It was as though she had been given permission to speak her truth for the very first tine. She began telling Genevieve all the things she wished for – her own business, her own home, a good life for her children. Her confusion cleared as her walls came tumbling down. In a startling declaration, she heard herself announce, "I'm finished playing small in life. I want to live with purpose, have a dream ... be more, do more, have more!" *"As You Wish!'*

It was a compelling, heartfelt statement. Both women felt its power. After a short while, Genevieve asked in her gentle way, "Is that it, then? Are you done?"

Hannah was touched by the simplicity of the two questions. "Yes," she answered.

Genevieve then reached into her purse. "I have something to give you." She placed a small object in Hannah's hand then closed it into a fist.

"Hannah, this is a gift to celebrate the end of your days as a victim of the people and the circumstances around you.

"You hold in your hand all you wish for in life – whatever you want it to be. What you think, you will create. So live with love and honor for yourself as a woman and with commitment to your vision. Choose friends who will support your dreams and remind you of what you want.

"Know without a doubt that you are capable of having whatever you want or the desire would not be there. Pursue your heart's desire with every thought, word, and action. Remember that as a woman thinks, so she becomes."

Hannah's eyes were filled with tears as she stood to leave, grasping the object in her hand as surely as she held the message in her heart.

In that very same instant, just a few deep breaths up the mountain at High Ground, Genie raised her joyous face up to the sky and sang, "Ahh, ha, Hannah! You hear it in your heart, the song that's all your own! Your thoughts are things that you create. Exactly As You Wish!"

And her whirling, swirling dance of lights whisked off into the Valley.

LATER THAT DAY ...

Hannah did not go to work after her conversation with Genevieve at the café. She canceled all her appointments and drove into the mountains with a backpack of supplies, including her dream journal and gratitude list. Being alone with her thoughts was all she wanted today.

She impulsively took a right turn and found herself on a winding, tree-lined road that ended at a meadow. She took her backpack and a blanket out of the car and walked into the open meadow. She stayed there for hours, feeling, writing, remembering, and gazing up at the vast blue sky.

She held in her hand the gift from Genevieve – a smooth rose quartz heart-shaped stone. It was a reminder of everything she wanted and all that she could be. She held it to her chest and thought about Aaron and Andra, wondering, "What are my children learning about life and love? What have I been teaching them?"

There was no question that a breakthrough had occurred in El Deseo. The whisper in Hannah's heart was now a mighty roar, a voice insisting to be heard.

As the afternoon grew long, Hannah knew it would soon be time to pick up Aaron and Andra at Maggie's house, so she gathered her things and returned to the valley. She still had enough time, though, to make a very important stop. She thought, "It's about time I started making things happen in my life!" "As You Wish!"

That evening Hannah and her small family had an unplanned celebration. It began when Hannah made an announcement: "Guess what? You know that big yellow house on the road that winds up toward the mountain?"

The twins nodded in unison. Andra said, "I love that house! It looks just like something in a fairy tale."

"Well, your mom signed a contract today to buy it, and soon it will be our new home! I decided to do something wonderful for us with my savings!" Andra screamed with joy and danced all around the apartment while Aaron repeated over and over again, "Too cool, Mom!"

Hannah and the kids giggled and played and shared their dreams throughout the evening. Just before bedtime, Hannah looked at the nightstand by her bed and saw the rose quartz heart she had received from Genevieve earlier that day. She decided to share the message with her son and daughter without delay.

Hannah sat at the end of the bed and had each of them hold out a hand. Then she told them to make a fist and asked, "Guess what's in your hands?" Aaron and Andra guessed with exaggerated facial expressions. "There's nothing in it!" and "My hand is empty!"

Hannah smiled, shook her head, and

made them guess some more. Then she grew quiet and told them, "In your hand is all you wish. Whatever you want to be. You are capable and worthy of creating whatever you want in your life."

The twins looked at their adolescent hands with wide-open eyes as the message sank in. That night was the happiest they had ever been.

Throughout the starry moonlit night, a few deep breaths up the mountain, the heart of Genie swelled with love for miracles and magic. "Ahh, Hannah, now you are discovering the power of living exactly As You Wish."

DAY FIVE

"I'm leaving early this morning to stop at Storytime Café. Be sure you catch your bus on time," Hannah reminded Aaron and Andra.

"Yeah, we will," they said as they bustled about their morning chores. "See you tonight." There was magic in the air, a new rhythm to their lives.

Hannah planned to spend the entire day taking action steps toward her new goals. She arrived at Storytime Cafe well before seven o'clock hoping to begin with one of Genevieve's innovative stories. As she entered she saw that Genevieve, Aimee, and Maggie were seated together at a table with one empty chair. They motioned for her to join them as soon as they saw her come in.

"You look very happy today," Genevieve observed.

"Rumor has it that you placed a contract on the High Ground House," Maggie added.

"High Ground House?" Hannah asked

with a puzzled look.

"Yes, that lovely yellow house is right on the road to High Ground Meadows. That's how it got its name."

"I didn't know! And, yes, it will be our new home!"

Then Hannah happily announced, "You can celebrate something else with me today if you'd like. I've decided to put all my focus and attention toward starting my own business! It's an idea I've been working on for awhile and, now I'm ready to implement a business plan and make it happen." "As You Wish!"

She enthusiastically shared her long-time dream of the unique concept she had developed.

"I call it 'Fast Track, Inc.' The purpose of the business is to provide entry level jobs for qualified candidates just graduating from high school. There will be incentives for the firms that use our services to help fund scholarships for skill training or college and personal development. They will step up from Track I to Track IV. Everyone will win! And I'll have the satisfaction of knowing I'm making a difference in the world!"

The four women clinked their coffee cups and cheered Hannah's big adventure. Then Aimee asked, "Hannah, what can we do to help you?"

Before Hannah could reply, Maggie jumped in saying, "C'mon, ladies. Between us we've started seven different businesses, five of which struck gold. Let's brainstorm Hannah's dream!"

And that's just what they did for the next three hours. The synergy moved from one woman to another in an endless stream of ideas.

"Above all," Genevieve concluded, "pay vigorous attention to every thought you have. Your subconscious mind is like a Genie. It does not distinguish between positive and negative, good and bad.

The Genie within takes every thought as a command and immediately goes to work to manifest it into physical reality. The hardest work you'll ever do is to think positive thoughts and hold on to your desires in spite of circumstances that may be around you ... and, of course at the same time, you must move your feet!"

Like a butterfly breaking out of her cocoon, Hannah grew stronger with each word.

And from that moment on, Hannah paid attention to her every thought and began living a truly abundant life ...

EXACTLY AS SHE WISHED!

FIVE YEARS LATER

Ahush fell over the audience as the Awards Chairman introduced the names and briefly described the achievements of the ten Horatio Alger Award recipients. Filled with gratitude and joy, Hannah sat with the five women and four men with whom she would share the prestigious award.

She looked out into the crowd of more than a thousand attendees and gazed lovingly upon the table at which her closest friends, family, and supporters were seated. Among them were Genevieve, Maggie, Aimee, and the twins, Andra and Aaron, now nearly eighteen years old and college-bound in the fall.

So much had been accomplished and there was so much more to be done! Fast Track, Inc. had grown into a coveted franchise opportunity with many offices scattered throughout several countries.

And, most near-and-dear to Hannah's heart, her dream to assist at-risk youth in finding entry level jobs to jumpstart their careers had grown into an enormous global network with unprecedented corporate support.

As Hannah's name was called, she approached the podium with confidence and grace. In a strong, clear voice she began to share her story ...

May all your New Beginnings be
EXACTLY AS YOU WISH!

HANNAH'S AFFIRMATIONS

I am courageous and fully capable of
living a life of abundance.

♥

I listen vigorously to my self-talk and replace
negative thoughts and words with positive
thoughts, words, and actions.

♥

I step out to do things I have never done in
order to have things I have never had.

♥

I greet every person with a silent wish
for their happiness, health,
and abundance.

♥

Money comes to and through me in
ever-increasing amounts enabling me to
give abundantly to myself, my family,
and my community.

I confidently carry more than enough money in order to have the liberty to meet my own wants and needs as well as those of my family.

♥

I trust myself and do not need the approval of others.

♥

I surround myself with positive people who support and empower me to be more, do more, and have more.

♥

I am grateful for all things, including adversity, knowing that there is opportunity for growth in every challenge.

♥

I am important. My every thought, word, and action makes a difference.

As Tina was driving to her office, the events of the morning as her children were getting ready for school weighed heavily upon her mind. She found herself thinking, "Maybe I should start carrying more cash in my purse. Why do I only carry a few dollars?"

You see, that particular morning was no different from a lot of other mornings when her three children were rushing off to school and asking her for money for lunch, school projects, yearbooks, field trips, etc. In the rush, she would grab her purse to see if she could find the money needed for school that day. "Wait a minute. I'll have to go get money from your dad's billfold," the kids heard her say. Or she'd tell them, "Go ask your dad for the money," knowing he always had cash.

What was she teaching her daughters, as well as her son, about women and money? The answer: Women don't have money. And how does that translate subliminally? The answer: Women are less capable, less responsible, less powerful. It didn't matter that Tina had a six figure income from her own business. She never carried more than $20 on any average day.

A survey was taken of 133 people of which nearly half were female. This particular group would not be considered "average" by most people. They were attending a wealth-consciousness program with other people sharing the common goal of becoming millionaires. Notice the difference in the results between the behaviors of these men and women with regard to money:

Question #1: On the average, how much cash do you carry in your wallet or billfold?
Response: Female (average) – $56.00
            Male (average) – $173.00
Note that 9% of the men vs. 37% of the women carried $20.00 or less.
Conclusion: Men carry approximately three times more cash than women.

Question #2: If you are married, what is the most money you have ever spent on a single item for yourself, children, spouse or household without first consulting your spouse?

Response: Female (average) – $2,446.00

Male (average) – $28,788.00

Conclusion: Men independently spend approximately twelve times more than women.

Question #3: If you are a single woman, how much do you think about the possibility that the more success-ful you become, the more intimidated men will be to ask you for a date? (Scoring: 1 = never think about it; 10 = think about it a lot)

Response: Average score = 7

Conclusion: Women are very concerned about the effect success will have on future potential relationships.

We learned that after the survey was taken some of the women left the meeting and made life-changing decisions based simply upon the new level of awareness they had achieved since participating in the survey. Thus, the reason for this book.

Our desire is that this modern-day fairy tale will be read by countless men and women who will then become aware of the limiting thoughts and beliefs which have been holding them back from being, doing, and having more.

Note that this conditioning, which is so prevalent among today's women, is not necessarily exclusive to women. The Genie, our subconscious mind, accepts whatever our conscious mind feeds it – positive or negative – and accepts it as reality. Whenever a thought is impressed upon it, the subconscious mind acts like the Genie and says, "As you wish," going to work to bring everything into harmony and alignment with that thought. Think of the analogy of a carrot seed. If you plant a carrot seed, it will not say, "I think I'll grow to be broccoli." It will become a carrot. Even so, you become the thought that you choose to plant in your mind. This gift is the God-given freedom of choice for which every individual is responsible.

Use the affirmations at the end of this book to replace negative thoughts and you, too, will know that you are capable and worthy of creating a life of abundance – As You Wish!

Carol and Tina